The Complete Gravy Cookbook

Great Yummy Gravy Recipes to Make Your Meals Tastier

By: Owen Davis

Copyright Notice!

Table of Contents

Introduction

Making the perfect gravy is something that everyone should know. So next time you're in the kitchen, whether it's a weekday morning or late at night, you'll be able to make up a delicious, wholesome, and healthy meal.

Gravy is one of the most delicious sauces that can be served with different types of food. It is made from the juices of meat or vegetables and is usually served over a side dish such as mashed potatoes or rice. Making gravy, however, is an art in itself -- it takes a bit of skill and practice to get the gravy just right.

In this book, you'll find that getting the most out of your gravy is as easy as can be. There's a wide variety of recipes for you to choose from, so that you can make yourself and others happy. All of the recipes are very easy to follow and are presented in an easily accessible format. So whether you're a beginner or an expert, there's something here for everyone.

The benefits of learning how to make gravy are numerous. It's a great way to impress your friends and family, or even use it as a subject for small talk at the dinner table. You'll also find that it's easy and convenient to prepare because you can make the gravy in advance and serve it over different types of food. You'll also find that serving a family dinner or having a party is much easier with the perfect gravy in your repertoire.

Alternatively, you can also present the gravy as a side dish to another meal. In this way, it can be served alongside other delicious dishes, making it even more convenient for you to prepare.

The recipes included in this book are perfect for everything from parties to weeknight dinners. With these delicious recipes, you'll be able to surprise everyone with something new, something they've never thought of or have tasted before. The only limit with these recipes is your imagination!

The book contains many detailed recipes for making a gravy. If you are new to cooking, this cookbook is a great place to start. Even if you don't plan to become a chef, learning a few basic recipes can help you save a lot of money and time. This is the perfect book for beginning cooks and will teach you to make the perfect gravy. So get one today and start cooking in your home today! You will thank yourself later!

Gravy Recipes

Some of these recipes are relatively simple, while others require more time and skill. Regardless of your skill level, you'll find that all of these recipes are easy to follow and will turn out great every time.

1. Southern Style Tomato Gravy

Do you crave a thick gravy? This Southern-style tomato gravy will leave you yearning for more. The bacon adds more taste to the creamy gravy.

Servings: 6

Preparation time: 30 minutes

Ingredients:

- 1 (1 lb.) package bacon
- 1 tsp. Butter
- 2 tbsps. Flour
- 2 (14 oz.) cans whole tomatoes
- 2 tsps. Salt
- 4 tsps. Ground black pepper
- 1 (3 oz.) package softened cream cheese
- ½ c. Heavy cream

Directions:

Cook bacon over moderate heat for 10 minutes in a skillet until browned evenly. Next, transfer it to a plate lined with a paper towel to drain as you reserve the drippings in the pan.

In the drippings, add butter and flour, then mix. Pickle the browned bits off your pan's bottom using a wooden spoon, then cook as you scramble for 3 minutes until the mixture thickens.

Next, add the tomatoes to the mixture, then use the spoon to break them into small pieces as you cook.

Add salt and pepper to the mixture, then add the cheese and heavy cream.

Reduce the heat, then let the mixture simmer for 10 minutes until it thickens as you stir frequently.

2. Sausage with Parsley Gravy

Spice up your breakfast by preparing this yummy sausage gravy. It takes a few minutes to prepare and cook.

Servings: 4

Preparation time: 13 minutes

Ingredients:

- 1 lb. Ground pork sausage
- ¼ c. Chopped onion
- 1 tsp. Garlic powder
- 1 tsp. Dried parsley
- ½ tsp. Salt
- ¼ tsp. Pepper
- 2 tbsps. All-purpose flour
- 1 c. Milk

Directions:

In a skillet over heat, sauté the onion and sausage for 10 minutes until the mixture becomes brown.

Add pepper, parsley, salt, and garlic powder to the sausage mixture to season.

Add flour to the stickiness of your desire, then pour in the milk until you get the consistency of your liking. Finally, heat the mixture for 3 minutes.

3. Simple Beef Flavored Gravy

Beef gravy goes well with many meals like bread and mashed potatoes. It is a three-step recipe making it easy to make.

Servings: 2

Preparation time: 8 minutes

Ingredients:

- 1½ c. Water
- 3 tsps. Beef bouillon
- ¼ c. All-purpose flour
- 1 chopped onion
- ¼ c. Butter

Directions:

Mix the flour, butter, bouillon, onion, and water in a saucepan.

Next, boil the mixture over moderate heat for 8 minutes until it thickens.

4. Chicken Gravy

The chicken gravy is tasty, and you will only need three ingredients to execute this recipe. So what's keeping you waiting? Try it today!

Servings: 4

Preparation time: 10 minutes

Ingredients:

- ½ c. All-purpose flour
- 1 c. Water
- 1 (3 lbs.) drippings from roasted chicken

Directions:

Add water onto the drippings until you get a total of 1½ cups of liquid at your roaster's bottom.

Add flour to the mixture to make it thick but not a pastry mixture. Whisk the flour and water mixture onto the drippings, set the roaster on medium heat, and place the roaster on the stove. Constantly stir until the mixture is bubbly and thickened. Season with salt and pepper to taste.

5. Sour Wiener Gravy

Do you love frankfurters? If yes, this gravy will have you wanting to have more and more. What's more, you don't have to be an excellent chef to make this gravy.

Servings: 6

Preparation time: 8 minutes

Ingredients:

- 5¾ c. Cold water
- 1 finely chopped onion
- 1 tsp. Salt
- 1 tsp. Pepper
- 30 crushed gingersnap cookies
- 1½ c. Distilled white vinegar
- 2 lbs. Sliced frankfurters

Directions:

Mix onion, gingersnap cookies, and cold water in a skillet. Mix gently until the cookies have completely dissolved.

Pour in sliced frankfurters and vinegar. Heat and simmer mixture over moderate heat until combination has become somewhat thick.

Serve gravy over warm mashed potatoes.

6. Onion Gravy for British Bangers and Mash

Onion gravy is a common type of gravy that most people prepare. So what is stopping you from getting into your kitchen to make this recipe?

Servings: 4

Preparation time: 50 minutes

Ingredients:

- 6 tbsps. Butter
- 3 thinly sliced onions
- 1 (14.5 oz.) can chicken stock
- 1 tbsp. All-purpose flour
- ½ c. Red wine
- 2 tsps. Dijon mustard
- 1 tsp. Worcestershire sauce
- ½ tsp. Salt
- ¼ tsp. Ground black pepper

Directions:

In a heavy-bottomed pan, liquefy butter over medium heat. In the liquefied butter, cook and mix onion for 10 minutes till softened.

Turn heat down to low. Next, cover your pan and cook for 20 minutes until onions are caramelized, mixing from time to time.

In the caramelized onions, mix flour and cook for a minute.

In the onion mixture, put Worcestershire sauce, Dijon mustard, chicken stock, and red wine; let simmer for 15 minutes till the sauce thickens, mixing often. Spice with black pepper and salt.

7. Parsley Mushroom Gravy

This blend of mushroom and parsley is worth your time for gravy lovers. You can serve it with any meal like mashed potatoes, rice, and bread.

Servings: 2

Preparation time: 10 minutes

Ingredients:

- 2 tbsps. Chicken drippings
- ¼ c. All-purpose flour
- 2 c. Chicken broth
- 1 c. Canned (drained) sliced mushrooms
- 1 tbsp. Finely chopped parsley
- ½ tsp. Salt
- ¼ tsp. Ground black pepper

Directions:

Over medium heat, heat the chicken drippings in a small saucepan. Add the flour and continue to cook for around 3 minutes, until the mixture is golden brown, while continuously stirring the mixture. Add the broth, then allow the mixture to boil.

Cook the mixture for 5 minutes until the gravy thickens as you stir the mixture continuously. Next, stir in mushrooms, parsley, salt, and pepper.

8. Perfect Brown Gravy

This gravy is so good that you can take it alone or with other meals. It is tasty and kicks the right spots.

Servings: 4

Preparation time: 10 minutes

Ingredients:

- 1¾ c. Water
- ¼ c. Beef drippings
- 2 (24g each) packages McCormick® Brown Gravy Mix

Directions:

In a medium saucepan, pour in beef drippings and water. Mix in the Gravy Mixes until the mixture has become smooth, using a wire whisk.

Frequently stir and cook the mixture on medium heat until it boils. Lower heat to low setting, and then simmer until thickened, which should take about a minute, while stirring gravy mixture occasionally. However, note that the gravy will continue to thicken while it stands.

9. Perfect Turkey Gravy

This gravy is a good thanksgiving gravy that can go with a range of other dishes. It is a healthy fix for the whole family.

Servings: 4

Preparation time: 15 minutes

Ingredients:

- 2 (.87 oz.) packages McCormick Turkey Gravy Mix
- ¼ c. Flour
- 3 c. Water
- 1 c. Turkey pan drippings
- 1 c. Cooked, chopped turkey giblets

Directions:

In a big saucepan, combine flour and Gravy Mix. Using a wire whisk, slowly mix in turkey drippings and water until smooth. Mix in chopped turkey giblets.

Whisking often, cook on medium-high heat until the gravy boils. Lower the heat to low, simmer until thickened for 5 minutes, whisking sometimes.

10. Mama's Tomato Gravy

This gravy is out of this world. You do not require unique ingredients to make this dish as the ingredients are available at supermarkets near you.

Servings: 2

Preparation time: 10 minutes

Ingredients:

- ¼ c. Bacon drippings
- 3 tbsps. All-purpose flour
- 2 c. Water
- ½ (6 oz.) can tomato paste
- ½ tsp. Salt
- ¼ tsp. Ground black pepper

Directions:

In a skillet over moderate heat, heat the bacon drippings. Mix in the flour and cook until lightly browned, stirring constantly.

Gradually pour the water into the flour mixture while continuously whisking. Mix in the tomato paste. Cook until the mixture starts to thicken. Reduce the heat, then let the mixture simmer for 5 minutes until it becomes thick.

Season the mixture with salt and pepper.

11. Mexican Gravy

Another way of preparing a tasty gravy is by following this Mexican style of preparation. Again, the results are excellent, and you get a thick gravy.

Servings: 4

Preparation time: 20 minutes

Ingredients:

- ½ c. Flour
- 2 tbsps. Chili powder
- 2 tsps. Onion powder
- 1 tsp. Dried Mexican oregano
- 1 tsp. Salt
- 6 tbsps. Vegetable oil
- 4 c. Water

Directions:

Mix chili powder, flour, onion powder, salt, and oregano in a bowl.

In a saucepan, add the oil, then heat it over low heat. Mix flour mixture into the heated oil and stir until smooth.

Gradually pour water into the mixture and mix to blend smoothly between each addition. Bring the mixture to a simmer for 5 minutes.

Remove the saucepan from heat, and then let the mixture cool for 10 minutes.

12. Microwave Chocolate Gravy

It is a simple gravy to make, and all chocolate lovers will love it. With just one step, your chocolate gravy is ready within 8 minutes.

Servings: 4

Preparation time: 8 minutes

Ingredients:

- 1½ c. White sugar
- 4 tbsps. All-purpose flour
- 3 tbsps. Unsweetened cocoa powder
- ½ tsp. Salt
- 3 c. Milk
- ¼ tsp. Vanilla extract

Directions:

Mix salt, cocoa, flour, and sugar together in a microwave-safe bowl. Mix in vanilla extract and milk. Microwave on high heat for 5 minutes overall with 30-second intervals, mixing between each, till gravy becomes thick.

13. Miso Gravy (Gluten-Free and Vegan)

It is a vegan and gluten-free gravy that is full of flavor. You will only need water, miso paste, liquid aminos, vegetable bouillon base, cornstarch, onion powder, and garlic granules.

Servings: 4

Preparation time: 20 minutes

Ingredients:

- 3 c. Water
- 1 tbsp. Miso paste
- 1 tbsp. Liquid aminos
- 1 tbsp. Vegetable bouillon base
- ¼ c. Cornstarch
- ¼ tsp. Onion powder
- ¼ tsp. Garlic granules

Directions:

In a saucepan, combine miso, water, bouillon base, and aminos over medium heat.

Sift onion powder, garlic, and cornstarch into the mixture and mix until there are no more lumps.

Simmer the mixture for 10 minutes until it thickens.

14. Lightning Gravy

It is a quick gravy fix that you can make in under 10 minutes. The taste is wow and will leave you yearning for more, so prepare enough.

Servings: 2

Preparation time: 8 minutes

Ingredients:

- 2 c. Hot water
- 2 (3 oz.) cubes chicken bouillon
- 2 tbsps. Cornstarch
- 1 tbsp. Cold water

Directions:

Pour water into a microwave-safe dish, add bouillon, and heat in the microwave on high power, until it boils, stirring occasionally.

In another bowl, mix cornstarch with cold water, then stir. Next, pour the mixture into the hot broth and cook in the microwave for 1 minute on medium power until it becomes thick as you stir every 30 seconds.

15. Homemade Chicken Gravy

This gravy is simple to prepare, resulting in a thick, tasty, and flavorful dish. It complements several dishes not limited to fries and mashed potatoes.

Servings: 4

Preparation time: 35 minutes

Ingredients:

- ½ c. butter, Unsalted
- ½ c. flour, all-purpose
- 4 c. Cold chicken stock
- 1/3 c. Heavy cream
- 1 tsp. Salt
- ¼ tsp. white pepper, ground
- ¼ tsp. Cayenne pepper

Directions:

Using a medium-low source of heat, heat butter in a saucepan. Mix in flour for around 12 minutes until fragrant.

Mix in cold stock gradually. Decrease the heat to low. Let gravy simmer, cooking and mixing for around 15 minutes until mixture is thick enough to coat a spoon's back. Mix in the heavy cream, and season with cayenne pepper, salt, and white pepper.

16. Easiest Delicious Red Wine Steak Sauce

This thick gravy goes well with barbeque meat and fries. You can use it as a dipping too.

Servings: 2

Preparation time: 15 minutes

Ingredients:

- 1 (.75 oz.) packet brown gravy mix, dry
- ½ c. Red wine
- ½ c. Cold water
- ¼ tsp. Garlic powder

Directions:

Add the red wine, brown gravy, and cold water to a saucepan. Season mixture with garlic powder.

Over medium heat, bring the gravy mixture to a boil. Mix for around one minute until the mixture has thickened.

17. Mom's Country Gravy

When you have vegetable oil, salt, milk, all-purpose flour, and black pepper, this recipe should be ringing in your mind. The preparation directions are only two, making it an easy fix when you have limited time.

Servings: 6

Preparation time: 20 minutes

Ingredients:

- ½ c. Vegetable oil
- 1 tsp. Salt
- 4 c. Milk
- ¾ c. All-purpose flour
- 1 tsp. Ground black pepper

Directions:

Heat a greased frying pan. Put flour, pepper, and salt in the hot oil until it gets smooth. Then, heat it for 10 minutes until it gets brown.

Keep stirring it to avoid lumps. Cook it until it becomes thick. Then, enjoy it with your family.

18. Country Sausage Gravy

The country sausage gravy is delicious and creamy. You can serve it with a lot of dishes like bread and mashed potatoes.

Servings: 4

Preparation time: 35 minutes

Ingredients:

- 1 lb. Pork sausage
- 1 chopped green bell pepper
- 2 tbsps. Minced garlic
- ½ tsp. Salt
- ¼ tsp. Pepper
- 1 tsp. Minced sage
- 2 c. Milk
- ¼ c. Minced parsley
- 1 chopped onion
- 1 tsp. Red pepper flakes
- 4 tbsps. Unsalted butter
- 4 tbsps. All-purpose flour
- 1 tsp. Minced thyme
- 2 (3 oz.) cubes Chicken bouillon

Directions:

Heat the pork, garlic, onion, red pepper flakes, and green pepper in a hot frying pan until the pork is tender. Remove extra fat but not all.

Add the pepper, butter, and salt to the onion mixture. Heat the mixture until the butter gets melted. Gradually, stir in the flour. Mix all together and heat it for 5 minutes. Stir constantly. Now, put the thyme as well as sage.

Add half a cup of milk one by one. Mix all together. The mixture will become thick. Now, stir in more milk. Don't boil it. Put in the chicken bouillon. Heat it for 5 minutes. When the mixture gets thick, pour more milk into it.

Before serving it, pour 1/4 cup of milk and parsley.

19. Savory Turkey Gravy

It is a spicy gravy that can serve to up to 24 people. It takes 20 minutes to prepare, with easy-to-follow directions.

Servings: 24

Preparation time: 20 minutes

Ingredients:

- 5 c. Turkey stock
- 1 c. Water
- 1 tsp. Salt
- ¼ tsp. Celery salt
- ¼ c. All-purpose flour
- 1 tsp. Poultry seasoning
- ½ tsp. Ground black pepper

Directions:

Boil the turkey stock in a skillet over medium heat. Put the flour in water in a mixing bowl and mix them well.

Now, pour the turkey stock into the flour mixture and combine well. Stir in the poultry seasoning, celery salt, pepper, and salt. Let them boil and then decrease the heat. Cook for 10 minutes until the gravy gets thick.

20. Red Eye Gravy with Ham

This gravy is tasty as it has cayenne pepper, ham scraps, salt, black pepper, ham, flour, and vegetable oil. Your whole family would love it.

Servings: 4

Preparation time: 30 minutes

Ingredients:

- 1 tbsp. Vegetable oil
- 1 tsp. All-purpose flour
- 1/8 tsp. Cayenne pepper
- 2/3 c. Brewed coffee
- ½ c. Chopped fatty ham scraps
- ½ tsp. Salt
- ¼ tsp. Black pepper
- 4 (¼" thick) Ham slices

Directions:

Add oil to the frying pan. Put the ham scraps in the hot frying pan and cook for 5 minutes until they get brown. Transfer to a bowl and reserve some grease.

Add the ham slices to the frying pan. Heat them for 5 minutes until they get brown. Sprinkle the salt, cayenne pepper, and black pepper on ham slices. Transfer the ham to a bowl.

Decrease the heat and put the flour in the frying pan drippings. Heat it for 2 minutes. Now, increase the heat and add the coffee to the frying pan. Whisk constantly. Heat it until it gets thick. Again, put the ham in the frying pan to become warm.

21. Southern Style Creamy Gravy

Tomato gravy is a typical recipe, but this southern-style gravy is unique. It is tasty and appealing to the eye.

Servings: 16

Preparation time: 35 minutes

Ingredients:

- 1 (1 lb.) package Bacon
- 2 tbsps. Flour
- 2 tsps. Salt
- 1 (3 oz.) package of Cream cheese
- 1 tsp. Butter
- 2 (28 oz.) cans of whole tomatoes
- 4 tsps. Ground black pepper
- ½ c. Heavy cream

Directions:

Heat bacon in a pan for 10 minutes until it gets brown. Reserve drippings in the pan. Sieve the bacon.

Put flour as well as butter in bacon drippings. Cook for 3 minutes until it starts to get thick. Add tomatoes to it and sprinkle pepper and salt. Pour heavy cream as well as cream cheese. Cook for 10 minutes until thick.

22. Roast Chicken Pan Gravy

It is a savory gravy that your family would love. It is an excellent recipe to try when you want to experiment in the kitchen.

Servings: 4

Preparation time: 15 minutes

Ingredients:

- ¼ c. Drippings from a roasted chicken
- 2 c. Cold chicken stock
- 2½ tbsps. All-purpose flour
- 1 tsp. Salt
- ¼ tsp. Ground black pepper

Directions:

Take a bowl and put the fat of drippings in it. Reserve the fat. Put the flour in the remaining drippings in the pot. Pour 2 tbsp. of the reserved fat into the pot.

Put the pot on the stove and fry the flour for 5 minutes until it gets golden.

Pour 1/3 cup of the cold chicken stock into the pot. Mix all together. Boil it. Cook for 10 minutes until the gravy gets thickened.

23. Gluten-Free Sausage Gravy

It is a yummy creamy gravy. The gravy is simple and quick to prepare.

Servings: 16

Preparation time: 35 minutes

Ingredients:

- 1 lb. Bulk pork sausage
- 10 tbsps. Gluten-free all-purpose baking flour
- 60 grinds (4 tsps.) divided Black pepper
- 1 tsp. Salt
- 1 c. Unsalted butter
- 1 tsp. Salt
- 6 c. Divided milk

Directions:

Heat a pan. Add sausage to the pan and cook for 5 minutes until brown. Sieve and remove grease. Decrease the heat to low.

Put the butter in the sausage to melt and add flour. Next, cook for 10 minutes. Sprinkle 1 tsp. of salt and thirty black peppers.

Increase the heat and add the milk. Let it boil. Cook for 10 minutes until the gravy gets thick.

24. Sausage Gravy with Buttermilk Biscuits

This gravy is so yummy that you will become addicted since the sausages add more taste. It takes only 25 minutes to prepare.

Servings: 8

Preparation time: 25 minutes

Ingredients:

- 1 lb. Pork sausage
- 4 c. Milk
- 16 Buttermilk biscuits
- 1/3 c. Flour
- ½ tsp. Pepper

Directions:

Heat the sausage in a pan.

Sieve the fat.

Put the flour on the sausage and mix all together well.

Heat the sausage for 5 minutes.

Pour the milk into the sausage.

Heat until it gets thick.

Sprinkle the pepper and serve the gravy over the biscuits.

25. Mushroom Cream Gravy Sauce

You can make this recipe for special occasions. Nonetheless, it is easy to prepare and goes with anything you like.

Servings: 6

Preparation time: 30 minutes

Ingredients:

- 3 tbsps. Butter
- 2 minced garlic cloves
- 1 tbsp. Minced rosemary
- 1 c. Heavy cream
- ¼ tsp. Black pepper
- 2 minced shallots
- 1 (4 oz.) package of sliced button mushrooms
- 6 tbsps. Divided white wine
- 1 tsp. Sea salt
- 1 tsp. Parmesan cheese

Directions:

Melt the butter in a pan. Add the minced shallots and garlic cloves to the pan, then cook them for 3 minutes. Next, put the rosemary and mushrooms and mix them well for 1 minute.

Add the 1/4 cup of white wine to the pan and heat for 5 minutes until the mushrooms get browned.

Pour 2 tbsp. of the white wine and cream into the pan. Heat the mixture for 5 minutes until the gravy gets thickened.

Sprinkle the pepper, Parmesan cheese, and salt over the gravy.

26. Heavy Cream Chicken Gravy

This gravy takes only 30 minutes to prepare and turns out to be super yummy. You need butter, chicken stock, salt, white pepper, all-purpose flour, heavy cream, and cayenne pepper.

Servings: 8

Preparation time: 30 minutes

Ingredients:

- ½ c. Unsalted butter
- 4 c. Cold chicken stock
- 1 tsp. Salt
- ¼ tsp. Ground white pepper
- ½ c. All-purpose flour
- 1/3 c. Heavy cream
- 1 tsp. Cayenne pepper

Directions:

In a pan, melt butter. Next, put the flour in the pan and cook for 10 minutes.

Stir in the cold stock. Decrease the heat. Boil it and cook until thickened for 15 minutes. Add the cayenne pepper, white pepper, salt, and heavy cream.

27. Japanese Mushroom Gravy

This Japanese gravy recipe will leave everyone in the dining room satisfied. It is thick and goes well with bread and rice.

Servings: 4

Preparation time: 25 minutes

Ingredients:

- ¼ c. Olive oil
- ½ c. Whole wheat flour
- ¼ lb. Sliced shiitake mushroom
- 2 tbsps. Thyme
- 4 c. vegetable stock
- 2 tbsps. Soy sauce
- 1 tsp. Apple cider vinegar
- 1 tsp. Sea salt
- ½ tsp. Ground black pepper

Directions

In a pot, add the oil and cook until heated.

Add the flour, mixing continuously until smooth.

Stir in the mushrooms, then cook the mixture for 6 minutes.

Stir in the soy sauce and stock and cook until boiling.

Cook for about 30 minutes, stirring frequently.

Stir in the apple cider vinegar, salt, and black pepper and remove from the heat.

Enjoy hot.

28. Nutty Garlic Gravy

Are you a nut lover? Then, this gravy recipe is worth dying for as it is a thick and tasty fix that you can have with a variety of meal selections.

Servings: 12

Preparation time: 1 hour

Ingredients:

- 1 tbsp. Oil
- 1 chopped onion
- 2 c. Raw cashews
- 3 crushed garlic cloves
- 2 tbsps. Flour
- 2 tbsps. Soy sauce
- 1 tsp. Salt
- ½ tsp. Pepper
- 2 c. Water

Directions:

In a skillet, heat the oil and stir fry the onion for about 7 minutes.

Stir in the cashews and cook until toasted completely.

Add the garlic, then cook for 1 minute.

Stir in the flour, then cook for 1 minute.

Add the water in 2 batches, stirring continuously until smooth.

Add 2 cups of water, soy sauce, salt, and pepper and simmer for 30 minutes.

Remove your skillet from the heat, then keep aside for 5 minutes to cool.

In a food processor, add the cashew mixture and pulse until smooth.

Enjoy hot.

29. Mushroom Tamari Gravy

There is always a magical thing that happens when you prepare any mushroom gravy. The results are excellent.

Servings: 8

Preparation time: 30 minutes

Ingredients:

- 1 tbsp. Extra-virgin olive oil
- 1 chopped onion,
- 2 minced garlic cloves
- 1½ c. Chopped cleaned portabella mushrooms
- 2¼ c. Vegetable broth
- 3 tbsps. Tamari
- ¼ tsp. Dried thyme leaves
- 1/8 tsp. Crumbled dried sage
- 1 tbsp. Cornstarch
- 2 tbsps. Water
- ½ tsp. Fresh ground pepper

Directions:

Add the oil over medium heat and cook until heated through in a pot.

Add the garlic and onion and cook for about 6 minutes, mixing occasionally.

Stir in the mushrooms, then cook for 9 minutes, mixing occasionally.

Stir in the tamari, thyme, sage, and broth, then cook for 10 minutes.

In a bowl, add water, then dissolve the cornstarch in it.

Add the cornstarch mixture into the pot, stirring continuously.

Cook for about 10 minutes, mixing occasionally.

Stir in the pepper, then remove your pot from the heat.

With a slotted spoon, remove the onion and mushrooms.

Enjoy hot.

30. Red Gravy

This red gravy takes a lot of time to prepare, so you should make it in advance. However, it is thick and tasty, too, and you and your loved ones are satisfied.

Servings: 20

Preparation time: 6 hours 35 minutes

Ingredients:

- 5 (14.5 oz.) cans Cento Italian tomatoes
- 6 garlic cloves
- 2 lbs. Cubed turkey
- 5 tsps. Virgin olive oil
- 1 tsp. Basil
- 1 tsp. Crushed red pepper flakes

Directions:

In a food processor, add the tomatoes and pulse until smooth.

Heat the oil and stir fry the garlic for about 30 seconds in a pan.

Add the turkey, pureed tomatoes, basil, and red pepper flakes and stir to combine.

Reduce the heat, then simmer the mixture for 6 hours.

Enjoy hot.

31. Creamy Gouda Lunch Box

This creamy gravy recipe is full of flavor from the chicken breasts and seasoning. It is one recipe you cannot afford to miss making.

Servings: 4

Preparation time: 20 minutes

Ingredients:

- 4 skinless chicken breasts, cut into strips
- 2 tbsp thyme
- 1 tsp. Salt
- ½ tsp. Pepper
- 2 tbsps. Butter
- 2 tbsps. Flour
- ½ c. Chicken broth
- ½ c. Milk
- 1 c. shredded gouda cheese
- 1 c. Cooked white rice

Directions:

Season the breasts with salt, thyme, and pepper.

Heat a greased pan and stir fry the chicken for about 12 minutes until entirely done.

In another pan, add the butter and cook until melted.

Stir in the flour and cook for about 2 minutes, stirring continuously.

Add ½ cup of the milk and broth and cook for about 3 minutes, stirring continuously.

Stir in the salt and pepper.

Add the cheese as you stir until it melts.

Remove from the heat.

Enjoy the chicken with a topping of the gravy and some cooked white rice.

32. Marjoram Wheat Gravy

Wheat and marjoram are the perfect mixes for making this gravy recipe. It turns out sweet and very appealing to the eye.

Servings: 4

Preparation time: 1 hour 7 minutes

Ingredients:

- 1 (2 oz.) head garlic
- 6 tbsps. Whole wheat pastry flour
- 1 tbsp. Olive oil
- 1 tbsp. Canola oil
- 2 c. Water
- 6 tsps. Soy sauce
- 1 tsp. Crumbled dried thyme leaves
- 1 tsp. Dried marjoram

Directions:

Set your oven to 350°F before doing anything else.

Add the garlic and top with about 2" of water in a baking dish.

Cook in the oven for 30 minutes.

Next, remove the garlic from the oven and keep it aside to cool.

Carefully remove the top of the garlic head.

Remove the skin of garlic cloves and place them into a bowl, discarding the skin.

With a fork, mash the garlic cloves.

In a pan, add the flour over medium heat and cook until fragrant, mixing continuously.

Add the oil, beating strenuously until well combined.

Set the heat to low and stir in the garlic.

Cook for about 2 minutes, mixing occasionally.

Stir in the herbs, soy sauce, and water and cook for about 20 minutes, mixing often.

33. Gravy Spice Mix for Gravies

It is a perfect recipe for children and adults as well. You need flour, salt, paprika, black pepper, poultry seasoning, and garlic salt.

Servings: 2

Preparation time: 20 minutes

Ingredients:

- 1 c. All-purpose flour
- 2 tsps. Garlic salt
- 1 tsp. Paprika
- 1 tsp. Ground black pepper
- ¼ tsp. Poultry seasoning
- ½ tsp. Salt

Directions:

For the gravy mix in a bowl, add all the ingredients and mix until well combined.

Transfer into an airtight container to store.

For the gravy: in a wok, add 2 tbsp of the unsalted butter over low heat and cook until melted.

Stir in 2 tbsp of the gravy mix and cook for about 2 minutes, mixing continuously.

Add 1 c. of the chicken broth, stirring continuously.

Add 1 c. of the milk and stir to combine.

Increase the heat to high, mixing continuously.

Set the heat to low, then cook for 5 minutes.

34. Easy Egg Gravy

Most recipes that have egg in the ingredients are always simple to prepare, hence this recipe's name. It takes less than 10 minutes, the taste kicks the right spots, and you will never get enough of it.

Servings: 2

Preparation time: 7 minutes

Ingredients:

- 2 eggs
- 1 tbsp. Butter
- 1 tbsp. Flour
- ¼ c. Whipping cream
- ½ c. Skim milk
- 1 tsp. Seasoned salt
- ½ tsp. Black pepper

Directions:

In a skillet, break both, then cook until eggs get slightly. Next, stir in the salt and pepper and remove from the heat.

With a slotted spoon, transfer the eggs into a bowl.

Add the butter over medium-low heat and cook until melted in the same skillet.

Slowly add the flour and stir until well combined.

Slowly add the whipping cream, then stir until well combined.

Add the skim milk a little at a time and stir to combine well.

Se the heat to medium-low and cook until just boiling.

Cook until the gravy becomes thick.

Chop the eggs, then stir them into the gravy.

Remove from the heat and enjoy.

35. 45-Minute Chicken with Gravy

This chicken-gravy recipe is delicious and takes precisely 45 minutes to prepare and cook. It would go well with rice.

Servings: 4

Preparation time: 45 minutes

Ingredients:

- 2 tbsps. Unsalted butter
- 1 cut whole chicken
- 1 tsp. Salt
- ½ tsp. Pepper
- ½ tsp. Rosemary
- 1 c. Hot chicken stock
- 2 1/3 c. Sour cream

Directions:

Set your oven to 325°F before doing anything else.

In an oven-proof, add the butter and cook until melted.

Add the chicken and cook until browned completely.

Add the rosemary, salt, pepper, and stock over the chicken.

Cook in the oven for 35 minutes.

Next, remove it from the oven, transfer the pan juices into a pan over high heat, and cook until it reduces to ½ cup.

Add the sour cream and stir to combine well.

Transfer the chicken onto a platter and enjoy a topping of the gravy.

36. Birmingham Gravy

You prepare this special gravy recipe with butter, onion, mushrooms, bouillon cube, hot water, cornflour, black pepper, and salt. The results are excellent and worth the cooking time.

Servings: 6

Preparation time: 15 minutes

Ingredients:

- 2 oz. Butter
- 1 chopped onion
- 4 oz. Sliced mushrooms
- 1 (3 oz.) bouillon cube
- 300 ml hot water
- 2 tbsps. Corn flour, blended with 1/8 c. cold water
- 1 tsp. Salt
- ½ tsp. Black pepper

Directions:

In a pan, add the butter and cook until melted.

Add the mushrooms and onion and cook for about 7-8 minutes.

Add the stock cube and hot water to a bowl and mix well.

Add the stock cube mixture into the pan and stir to combine.

Stir in the cornflour mixture, then cook as you mix continuously until desired thickness.

Enjoy hot.

37. Mexican Chocolate Gravy

It is a thick delicious chocolate gravy that you prepare in a Mexican way. The steps are simple to comprehend and follow.

Servings: 4

Preparation time: 20 minutes

Ingredients:

- 1/3 c. Unsweetened cocoa powder
- 3 tbsps. all-purpose flour
- 2/3 c. Powdered sugar
- 1 tsp. Vanilla
- 2 c. Whole milk
- 2½ tbsps. Butter
- ¼ tsp. Salt
- ½ tsp. Cayenne pepper

Directions:

In a wok set on medium-low heat, melt butter.

Slowly add the flour, beating continuously until smooth.

Add the sugar and chocolate and beat until well combined.

Cook for about 2 minutes, stirring continuously.

Slowly add the milk, beating continuously until smooth.

Stir in cayenne, salt, and vanilla and cook for about 4 minutes.

Enjoy hot.

38. White Sausage Gravy

This Southern specialty is creamy and has a thick gravy. Traditionally, you can serve the gravy over biscuits.

Servings: 6

Preparation time: 20 minutes

Ingredients:

- 1 lb. Jones No Sugar Pork Sausage Roll sausage
- 2 tbsps. Finely chopped onion
- 6 tbsps. All-purpose flour
- 4 c. 2% milk
- ½ tsp. Rubbed sage
- ¼ tsp. Salt
- ½ tsp. Nutmeg
- ½ tsp. Hot pepper sauce
- 12 split warm biscuits

Directions:

Over moderate heat, cook the onion and sausage until the sausage is no longer pink in a skillet. Reserve 2 tbsps. of drippings in skillet and drain the rest.

Mix flour into drippings and sausage until blended. Cook and stir until it turns light golden brown.

Stir in seasonings and milk gradually and let it boil. Cook for 2 minutes as you stir until it thickens, and serve over biscuits.

39. Thanksgiving Gravy

It is a gray recipe full of flavor and a traditional type of gravy recipe. It serves four, but you can adjust the ingredients to your liking to accommodate more or less.

Servings: 4

Preparation time: 1 hour 40 minutes

Ingredients:

- 4 Turkey giblets and neck bone
- 2 c. Chicken broth
- 2 finely chopped carrots
- 1 chopped celery rib
- 2 finely chopped shallots
- 1/3 c. Cornstarch
- 3 c. Cold water
- ¼ c. Turkey drippings
- 2 tsps. Chicken bouillon granules
- ½ tsp. Pepper

Directions:

In a big saucepan, put shallots, celery, carrots, broth, neck bone, and the giblets; boil. Lower heat; put the cover and allow to simmer for 1¼ hours.

Filter and get rid of vegetables, neck bone, and giblets; reserve cooking juices. Mix water and cornstarch in a separate big saucepan till smooth; mix in bouillon and the drippings until smooth.

Little by little, mix in the leftover cooking juices. Boil; cook and mix till thickened, about 2 minutes. Add pepper to taste.

40. Tangy Cranberry Gravy

This gravy takes more time to prepare, but the outcome is worth the time. It is different from most recipes and very delicious too.

Servings: 3

Preparation time: 1 hour 30 minutes

Ingredients:

- 1 can (14 oz.) beef broth
- 3 Turkey giblets (liver removed)
- 2 tbsps. Cornstarch
- 1 tbsp. sugar
- ¾ c. Cranberry juice
- 1 tbsp. Cider vinegar
- 1 tbsp. Butter

Direction

Boil giblets and broth in a small saucepan. Lessen heat and simmer for about an hour, covered. Strain broth and then discard giblets; set aside.

Combine sugar, cornstarch, vinegar, and cranberry juice in another saucepan, and mix until smooth. Mix in butter and broth gradually.

Let the mixture boil and cook and mix gravy until thickened, taking about 2 minutes.

41. Creamy Tomato Gravy

This tomato gravy is creamy and rich with the bacon taste. You can serve it with cheesy grits, cornbread, eggs, or over biscuits.

Servings: 8

Preparation time: 35 minutes

Ingredients:

- 1 (1 lb.) package of bacon
- 1 (14 oz.) can whole tomatoes
- 1 tsp. Butter
- 2 tbsps. Flour
- 1 tsp. Pepper
- 2 tsps. Salt
- 1 (3 oz.) package cream cheese
- ½ c. Heavy cream

Directions:

Cook the bacon for 10 minutes in a skillet until browned evenly. Next, drain the bacon by placing it on a paper towel. Allow it to drain as you reserve the drippings in the pan.

Mix flour and butter into the drippings of bacon.

Using a wooden spoon, remove the browned bits by scraping them off the bottom of the pan; cook and mix for around three minutes until the mixture begins to thicken.

Mix tomatoes into the mixture, break them into smaller pieces with a spoon while cooking; and then season with pepper and salt.

Pour in heavy cream and cream cheese, decrease the heat setting to a medium-low, and let the mixture simmer for around ten minutes until it thickens and turns hot while stirring frequently.

42. Seasoned Garlic Gravy

This seasoned garlic gravy recipe is not only simple to make, but it is a tasty one with poultry seasoning. You can enjoy this gravy with turkey and mashed potatoes.

Servings: 2

Preparation time: 15 minutes

Ingredients:

- 3 tbsps. Butter
- 1 tsp. Minced garlic
- ¼ c. All-purpose flour
- ½ tsp. Poultry seasoning
- 1/8 tsp. Pepper
- 2 c. Chicken broth

Directions:

In a saucepan, add butter, then melt it.

Next, add garlic, cook, and mix for 1 minute.

Mix in the poultry seasoning, flour, and pepper until the mixture is smooth while whisking in broth gradually.

Bring mixture to a boil, continuously stir; cook for about 2 minutes.

43. Simple Beef Flavored Gravy

An easy and quick gravy that you make using beef bouillon. The steps are only two meaning that it takes a short time to prepare.

Servings: 6

Preparation time: 15 minutes

Ingredients:

- 1½ c. Water
- 3 tsps. Beef bouillon
- ¼ c. All-purpose flour
- 1 chopped onion
- ¼ c. Butter

Direction

Mix bouillon, onion, flour, butter, and water in a saucepan.

Next, boil over medium heat and cook until the mixture thickens.

44. Simple Chicken Gravy with Seasoning

Making this recipe is simple as you only need to follow the easy instructions after roasting your chicken. The outcome is satisfying and healthy too.

Servings: 4

Preparation time: 15 minutes

Ingredients:

- ½ c. All-purpose flour
- 1 c. Water
- ¼ tsp. Pepper
- ½ tsp. Salt
- 1 (2 lbs.) drippings from roasted chicken

Direction

Pour water onto the chicken drippings to measure 1½ cups of liquid at the bottom of the roaster.

Mix in water with the flour to make a thick yet not pasty mixture. Whisk the flour and water mixture onto the drippings, set the roaster on medium heat, and place the roaster on the stove. Constantly stir until the mixture is bubbly and thickened. Season with salt and pepper to taste.

45. Sour Wiener Gravy

It is a unique gravy recipe with sliced frankfurters. You can serve it with mashed potatoes or rice and enjoy it with the whole family.

Servings: 15

Preparation time: 35 minutes

Ingredients:

- 5¾ c. Cold water
- 1 finely chopped onion
- 3 tsps. Salt
- 2 tsps. Pepper
- 30 crushed gingersnap cookies
- 1½ c. Distilled white vinegar
- 2 lbs. Sliced frankfurters

Directions:

Mix onion, gingersnap cookies, and cold water in a large, deep skillet. Mix gently until the cookies have completely dissolved. Pour in sliced frankfurters and vinegar.

Heat and simmer mixture over low heat until mixture has become somewhat thick. Serve gravy over warm mashed potatoes.

46. Pantry Mushroom Gravy

This gravy is delicious and goes well with meatloaf, rice, or mashed potatoes. What's more, you can find the ingredients in the local stores next to you.

Servings: 2

Preparation time: 30 minutes

Ingredients:

- 1 (4 oz.) can of mushroom stems and pieces
- 3 tbsps. Butter
- ¼ c. Finely chopped onion
- 3 tbsps. All-purpose flour
- 1 tsp. Beef bouillon granules
- 1/8 tsp. Pepper
- ½ tsp. Browning sauce

Directions:

Drain mushrooms, and set aside liquid. Put sufficient water into the mushroom liquid to reach 1¼ cups.

Heat butter over medium-high heat in a small saucepan. Put in onion; cook and mix till soft. Mix in pepper, bouillon, and flour till blended. Put in mushrooms.

Slowly mix in the mushroom liquid mixture. Boil, mix continuously; cook until the gravy thickens, about 2 minutes. Mix in browning sauce if wished.

47. Orange Tarragon Gravy

It is a gravy with a distant sweetness of orange juice with a tarragon flavor. You can take it as it is or take it with other meals.

Servings: 2

Preparation time: 40 minutes

Ingredients:

- ½ c. Turkey drippings
- ¼ c. All-purpose flour
- ½ c. Orange juice
- 1 tsp. Chicken bouillon granules
- ¾ tsp. Minced fresh tarragon
- 1/8 tsp. White pepper

Direction:

Pour the drippings and their loosened browned bits into a measuring cup (2-cup). Skim fat from the mixture. Add just enough water to the drippings mixture to make 1½ cups.

Mix orange juice and flour in a small saucepan until smooth. Mix in the dripping mixture gradually. Stir in the pepper, tarragon, and bouillon. Bring the drippings mixture to a boil and continue to cook until it thickens, which should be for about two minutes.

48. Mushroom Sour Cream Gravy

You can make this recipe from mushrooms and leftover turkey. The steps are easy to follow along, and the results are excellent.

Servings: 4

Preparation time: 40 minutes

Ingredients:

- 1 lb. Thinly sliced fresh mushrooms
- 6 tbsps. Divided butter
- 1 finely chopped onion
- 2 chopped celery ribs
- 1/3 c. All-purpose flour
- ¾ tsp. Salt
- ¾ tsp. Pepper
- 2 c. Water
- ½ c. Sour cream

Directions:

In batches, sauté mushrooms in 3 tbsps. butter in a big skillet; reserve. Sauté celery and onion in 1 tbsp. butter using the same pan. Put in the rest of the butter, pepper, salt, and flour; cook and mix till smooth.

Slowly put in water. Boil; cook and mix till thickened, about 2 minutes. Mix in mushrooms and heat through. Take away from heat; mix in sour cream.

49. Kettle Gravy

You can also use this recipe to thicken the juices when you cook braised meats. It also takes a short time to make.

Servings: 3

Preparation time: 20 minutes

Ingredients:

- 2 c. Pan juices
- 6 tbsps. All-purpose flour
- 2/3 c. Cold water
- 1 c. Water
- ½ tsp. Salt
- ¼ tsp. Pepper

Directions:

Return pan juices to the roasting pan or pour them onto a saucepan. Mix in water and flour until smooth, and then stir the mixture into the pan juices.

Bring mixture to a boil, then cook for 2 minutes as you stir until thickened. Season the mixture with salt and pepper.

50. Herbed Pumpkin Gravy

It is a versatile gravy recipe that complements various food types. So what are the odds that you will love it? 10/10, I would say!

Servings: 10

Preparation time: 40 minutes

Ingredients:

- 1 c. Quick-cooking steel-cut oats
- 3 c. Water
- 2 c. Hot water
- 1 (15 oz.) can pumpkin puree
- 1 tsp. White sugar
- ½ tsp. Herbes de Provence
- ½ tsp. Salt
- 1/8 tsp. Ground black pepper
- ¼ tsp. Garlic powder
- 1 tbsp. Virgin olive oil

Directions:

In a saucepan, mix oats into 3 cups of water; boil, lower heat to low, and simmer for 20 minutes till the oats are soft and the water is absorbed.

Into the cooked oats, mix 2 cups of hot water. Filter water into a big saucepan as 'oat broth.' Reserve cooked oats for other use.

With a whisk, mix garlic powder, black pepper, salt, Herbes de Provence, sugar, and pumpkin puree into the oat broth till smooth; put in olive oil and mix to incorporate. Put additional hot water to thin the gravy, if wished. Over medium heat, put the saucepan, simmer gravy, and cook for 10 minutes till hot.

51. Giblet Turkey Gravy

Your family will love this gravy with wine and sage. The taste is heavenly, and the gravy is satisfying too.

Servings: 16

Preparation time: 25 minutes

Ingredients:

- ¼ c. Cornstarch
- 4 c. Divided chicken stock
- 1 tbsp. Butter
- 1 tbsp. Olive oil
- Finely chopped Giblets from 1 turkey
- ½ c. Dry white wine
- 2 tbsps. Minced fresh sage
- ¼ tsp. Alt
- ¼ tsp. Pepper

Directions:

Mix ½ cup of stock and cornstarch in a small bowl until smooth. Over medium-high heat, heat oil and butter in a big saucepan. Put giblets; for 8 minutes, cook, and stir until browned.

Add sage and wine to the pan. For 5 minutes, let it cook and stir for browned bits from the pan to loosen. Put leftover stock, then bring to a boil. Next, stir the cornstarch mixture, then return to a boil.

Next, reduce the heat, then simmer for 5 minutes as you stir the mixture occasionally until thickened to desired consistency. Finally, stir pepper and salt into the mixture.

52. Creamy Turkey Gravy

It is an easy recipe that even you, as a first-timer, won't have difficulty with when preparing it. For only 20 minutes, you will assemble this magical gravy.

Servings: 2

Preparation time: 20 minutes

Ingredients:

- 2 tbsps. Cornstarch
- 2 tbsps. Turkey drippings
- 1/8 tsp. Salt
- 1/8 tsp. Pepper
- 2 c. Chicken broth
- ¼ c. Whole milk

Directions:

Mix drippings, pepper, salt, and cornstarch in a small-sized saucepan.

Whisk in milk and broth gradually.

Bring the mixture to a boil as you stir it continuously, cook for 2 minutes, and mix until the mixture becomes thick.

53. Garbanzo Bean Gravy

Garbanzo bean gravy is a delicious vegetarian gravy substitute with very little fat but full of protein. You can adjust the ingredients to your liking to accommodate more.

Servings: 12

Preparation time: 45 minutes

Ingredients:

- 4 c. Water
- 1 minced onion
- 1½ c. Garbanzo beans, drained & rinsed (reserve liquid)
- 1 tsp. Salt
- ½ tsp. Dried basil
- ½ c. Soy sauce
- 1 tsp. Poultry seasoning
- 1 c. All-purpose flour

Directions:

Over high heat, bring onions and water to a boil in a saucepan. Turn heat to low, then simmer for 10 minutes until onions are very tender.

Meanwhile, puree the garbanzo beans in a blender using as much reserved liquid as needed to achieve a smooth puree. Then, stir the garbanzo puree into the mixture of the onions and the poultry seasoning, soy sauce, basil, and salt.

Mix in the flour until incorporated. Blend the gravy using an immersion blender until smooth.

Put the gravy back to a simmer. Turn the heat to low and cover, then simmer for 20 minutes as you stir the mixture frequently.

54. Ginger Ale Gravy

You can make this amazing ginger ale gravy for less than ten minutes. You will need the ginger ale, garlic cloves, red onion, lemon juice, salted butter, flour, pepper, and salt.

Servings: 2

Preparation time: 8 minutes

Ingredients:

- 450 ml ginger ale
- 2 finely minced garlic cloves
- 1 finely chopped red onion
- 1 tbsp. Fresh lemon juice
- 25 g salted butter
- 25 g Plain Flour
- ½ tsp. Salt
- ¼ tsp. Pepper

Directions:

Gently sauté the onion and garlic on a low to medium heat until the onion is translucent. Add the flour as you stir the mixture well for a minute.

Add the ginger ale and lemon juice, constantly thickening and removing any lumps.

Season to taste and keep warm on a low heat until you are ready to serve.

55. Herb and Ale Gravy

It is a healthy gravy good for your children and the whole family. The seasoning adds more taste to the whole dish.

Servings: 3

Preparation time: 20 minutes

Ingredients:

- 300 g finely chopped onions
- 4 finely minced garlic cloves
- 30 ml olive oil
- 300 ml English ale
- 1 chicken stock cube
- 10 g sweet paprika
- 15 g dried Sage
- 15 g dried Rosemary
- 5 g English Mustard Powder
- ¼ tsp. Salt
- ¼ tsp. Pepper

Directions:

Gently sauté onions and garlic in the olive oil for a few minutes, then add the spices, herbs, ale, and stock cube.

Bring the onion mixture to a boil, then reduce the heat. Simmer until the gravy reduces by half.

Pass the gravy through a fine sieve, then add salt and pepper to season. Finally, bring it back up to temperature before serving.

56. Leek and Apple Gravy

Looking for a quick gravy recipe, you can prepare for two? It is the ideal recipe as it guarantees good flavor and taste.

Servings: 2

Preparation time: 15 minutes

Ingredients:

- 200 g thinly sliced bacon bits
- 25 g Butter
- 1 thinly sliced leek, only the white part
- 1 tbsp. Plain flour
- 300 ml dry cider
- 3 peeled & cored apples
- 1 tbsp. Chopped flat-leaf parsley
- ½ tsp. Salt
- ¼ tsp. Pepper

Directions:

Gently sauté the bacon and the leek in the butter until the leek is cooked but not brown.

Stir the flour into the bacon and leek. Cut the apples into 6mm cubes and add them to the pan along with the cider.

Bring to the boil, then simmer as you stir until the gravy begins thickening.

Conclusion

There are many recipes that are included in this cookbook, so it can be hard to decide which ones you want. There's a variety of recipes you can try, and if you like one, there's a good chance you will like the others as well.

Are you ready to learn how to make delicious gravy? This cookbook is the perfect tool to help you start cooking in the kitchen. It's packed with detailed recipes and presented in an enjoyable format. Whether you are a beginner or an expert, there's something here for everyone!

About the Author

Owen isn't your typical cookbook writer. He built a life and career as a successful stockbroker in New York for many years, getting into the routine of it all. He enjoyed the crazy schedule, his exploding inbox, and endless phone conversations with clients. Still, he always found himself in the kitchen when he had some time to spare. Even if he got home at 11:00 pm and had an early morning meeting the next day, he always cooked delicious meals and dinners for himself.

When the pandemic hit and lots of his clients started pulling out, Owen began to question whether he would even have a job within the next couple of months. Once the world went into lockdown, his job became harder with the sudden obstacles of working from home with a job like his. His stress, however, was very fruitful because it often resulted in new dishes.

More than a home office, at one point, his place felt more like a restaurant. Whether it was breakfast, lunch, or dinner, he was always whipping up something amazing! When he was let go, he was relieved to finally have more time to work on new recipes to share with his friends and family. Eventually, they encouraged him to start writing cookbooks… and that's how he began his new life as an amateur cook and cookbook writer. Now, he travels across the US searching for inspiration for his recipes, but he always finds his way back home to his cozy townhouse in New Jersey, ready to share all of his new dishes with his loved ones.

Appendices

Hey, guys! I just wanted to say thanks for supporting me by purchasing one of my e-books. I have to say—when I first started writing cookbooks, I didn't have many expectations for myself because it was never a part of "the plan." It was more of a hobby, something I did for me and decided to put out there if someone might click on my book and buy it because they liked my food. Well, let me just say it's been a while since those days, and it's been a wild journey!

Now, cookbook writing is a huge part of my life, and I'm doing things I love! So, THANK YOU for trusting me with your weekly meal preps, weekend BBQs, 10-minute dinners, and all of your special occasions. If it weren't for you, I wouldn't be able to concentrate on producing all sorts of delicious recipes, which is why I've decided to reach out and ask for your help. What kind of recipes would you like to see more of? Are you interested in special diets, foods made with kitchen appliances, or just easy recipes on a time-crunch? Your input will help me create books you want to read with recipes you'll actually make! Make sure to let me know, and your suggestions could trigger an idea for my next book…

Take care!

Owen

Printed in Great Britain
by Amazon

13707520R00075